POLICE WORK

By Tami B. Morton

CELEBRATION PRESS
Pearson Learning Group

Contents

What Police Do

Did you know that about 600,000 men and women work as police officers in the United States? Some work for cities. Others work for counties or states. They all have a common goal, however. That's to keep people and their families safe.

These new police officers will be called on to do many different jobs.

Police officers are often called to the scene of traffic accidents.

Police officers make sure the laws, or the rules, are obeyed. They look into **crimes** carefully and arrest **criminals**. They also help find lost people, end quarrels, and help people who have been in accidents.

On Patrol

Most officers who wear uniforms patrol certain neighborhoods and communities. They wear uniforms so people will spot them easily and talk to them if they need help.

Police Officer's Clothing and Equipment

Hat

Radio

Uniform

Badge

Nametag

Police officers use two-way radios to find out about problems occurring on their beats.

Some officers are given a special beat, or area, to patrol. When officers patrol, they help people with many different types of problems, such as people who are in trouble or have been in an accident. They also try to stop crimes.

Police officers patrol their beat in different ways. Some officers walk their beat. They have smaller areas to patrol, so people get to know them better.

Many police officers ride in squad cars. These cars have a siren, a two-way radio, and often a computer. They can travel farther to help more people.

In many cities police officers ride motorcycles. The motorcycles can go places cars can't go. On the highway they can move in and out of traffic easily.

Some police officers ride bicycles on their beat. Like motorcycles, bicycles can go places cars can't. Officers can ride into narrow alleys and side streets. They can go up and down stairs. Bikes also allow officers to stop easily and talk to people in the community.

Mounted police officers ride horses. These officers patrol places like parks and mountain areas that are hard to get into by car. They also help control large crowds of people at special events, such as parades and concerts.

Mounted police help to control crowds.

Police in helicopters can cover wide areas.

Helicopters help police to find **suspects** traveling in cars and boats and on foot. The helicopters have huge spotlights and special cameras, which help police see better at night. Helicopters are used mostly by large cities or during **disasters**.

Solving Crimes

Some police officers are called detectives. Detectives **investigate**, or gather facts about, crimes. They usually do not wear uniforms because they want to catch criminals in the act.

Detectives are often called plainclothes officers because they do not wear uniforms.

A detective questions a woman about a robbery.

After a crime occurs, detectives go to the crime scene right away. They look at everything and take lots of photographs. They also ask **witnesses** lots of questions and look for as many pieces of **evidence**, or clues, as possible.

A police officer checks for fingerprints.

Detectives first look for **fingerprints** at the crime scene. They place each small object that has a fingerprint into a plastic bag. Scientists at the police laboratory study the prints and try to match them to others on record.

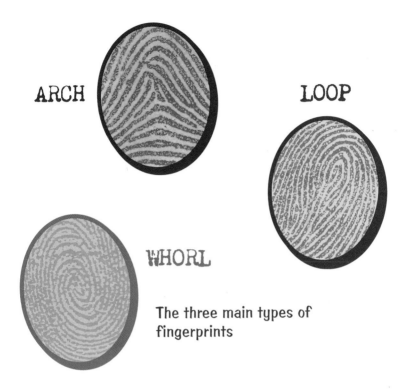

ARCH

LOOP

WHORL

The three main types of
fingerprints

Fingerprints are one of the most
important tools for the police.
Fingerprints are sorted into three main
types. The types are the arch, the loop,
and the whorl. No two people have
exactly the same fingerprints.

Police study clues, such as this piece of hair, to solve crimes.

If the police cannot find fingerprints, then hair, footprints, or clothing can be a clue. The police study each clue carefully. They can discover facts about the criminal from just about anything at the crime scene.

Special Police Units

Many police departments have special police units. These units, or teams, work on one type of problem or crime that occurs in the community. The officers on these teams get special training.

Officers on the SWAT team are trained to use special weapons.

Search and Rescue Team A search and rescue team looks for people lost in places, such as forests or caves. They practice skills like rock climbing to help them do their jobs better.

Special Weapons Unit Large cities often have a SWAT team. SWAT stands for *Special Weapons And Tactics.*
   The SWAT team is called when a criminal is armed, or carrying weapons. This team must know how to use many kinds of powerful weapons. They are trained to capture a criminal with little or no harm done to other people nearby.

Port Authority Police Team This team works mostly at airports, bridges, tunnels, and ports. They have many duties because they must protect people on land and in the water.

The Port Authority team uses boats to patrol the water.

The Port Authority team that serves the New York and New Jersey area is the oldest Port Authority team in the United States. Their job includes making sure the laws are obeyed, fighting fires, and doing rescue work.

K-9 Team Another important unit is the K-9 team. K-9 stands for "canine," which refers to the dog family. On this special team, officers work with police dogs. The dogs learn many skills to help officers fight crime or find people.

At K-9 training schools police dogs practice climbing and jumping over objects.

Police officers use dogs for many reasons. Dogs can run very fast. They also have a very good sense of smell. A dog can smell something in the air, on the ground, or inside a locker. Dogs can hear much better than people, too. Police dogs are trained carefully to use their skills to help police.

Some police dogs help officers on patrol. The dogs can catch criminals who try to run away and can find lost people.

Other dogs help detectives. These dogs learn to smell a certain scent. Some learn to find drugs. Other detective dogs are trained to find bombs. Some are also taught to find things that start fires, such as gasoline. Dogs may also learn to search for people buried under dirt and rocks after earthquakes or floods.

Helping Young People

Often, more than half of an officer's day is spent with people who are not criminals. Besides fighting crime many officers spend time with young people in their area. They want to help kids become good citizens.

Police officers often visit schools to teach children about safety and being good citizens.

Many police departments display the
D.A.R.E. letters on their squad cars.

Many officers take part in the D.A.R.E.,
or Drug Abuse Resistance Education,
program. Sergeant Letitia Huffstutler of the
Montville Township Police Department in
New Jersey says, "The program not only
teaches kids about the dangers of drugs. It
discusses ways to deal with peer pressure."

Police officers also give their time to other groups. In hundreds of cities in the United States, the police department runs the Police Athletic League, or PAL. The PAL often provides a meeting place and many programs for young people in their area.

Officers in PAL want to keep kids off the streets. They believe that kids are more likely to get into trouble if they do not have things to do that are fun.

PAL has many different programs for kids. It offers sports, music, dance, art, and drama. Children can take part in the programs after school or in the summer.

Other officers give their time to the Boys and Girls Clubs. They work with young people and provide programs that are fun and educational.

Remember, the police are always ready to help you.

The police work hard to protect families and catch criminals. You can help to make their job easier, though. Follow rules at school and at home. Then, you will become a good citizen. That's what police need most in their communities.

Glossary

crime	an act that is against the law
criminal	a person who breaks the law or commits a crime
disaster	a sudden event that brings great damage or loss
evidence	something, such as a piece of clothing, that can be used as proof of a crime
fingerprint	a mark left by a fingertip, showing the pattern of lines on its surface
investigate	to look into carefully and gather facts
patrol	to cover a certain area, usually on foot or in a car, to guard it
suspect	a person who is thought to have committed a crime
witness	a person who has seen an event and can tell what happened